11/10

Discover the
Dinosaurs

MEAT-EATING DINOSAURS

By Joseph Staunton
Illustrated by Luis Rey

amicus
mankato, minnesota

Published by Amicus
P.O. Box 1329, Mankato, Minnesota 56002

Printed in the United States of America at Corporate Graphics,
in North Mankato, Minnesota.

Published by arrangement with the Watts Publishing Group Ltd., London.

Library of Congress Cataloging-in-Publication Data
Staunton, Joseph.
  Meat-eating dinosaurs / by Joseph Staunton ; illustrated by Luis Rey.
      p. cm. -- (Discover the dinosaurs)
  Summary: "Profiles meat-eating dinosaurs from the Devonian, Triassic,
  Jurassic, and Cretaceous periods"--Provided by publisher.
  Includes index.
  ISBN 978-1-60753-109-8 (hardcover)
  1. Dinosaurs--Juvenile literature. 2. Carnivora, Fossil--Juvenile
literature. 3. Paleontology--Mesozoic--Juvenile literature. 4. Paleontology--
Devonian--Juvenile literature. I. Rey, Luis, ill. II. Title.
  QE861.5.S735 2011
  567.9--dc22

                                       2009028237

Editor: Jeremy Smith
Design: Simon Borrough
Art director: Jonathan Hair
Consultant: Dougla Dixon MSc
Illustrations: Copyright © Luis Rey 2008

All the words in the glossary appear in **bold** the first time they appear in the book.

1209
32010

Contents

A World of Dinosaurs

The world we live in is around 4.5 billion years old. Scientists know that there has been life on Earth for around 3.6 billion years because of **fossils** they have found. Some of these fossils were creatures called **dinosaurs**.

The Age of the Dinosaurs

Dinosaurs were the most famous group of animals to exist in **prehistoric** times. They included the largest land-living creatures that have ever lived. Alongside them lived many smaller, bird-like dinosaurs, monsters of the oceans, and massive flying **reptiles**. We know about dinosaurs because of the fossil remains they left behind. They lived in different periods of time, shown in the time line below and the one on page 31.

A Changing World

The Earth at the beginning of the age of the dinosaurs was very different from how it looks now. It was made up of one **supercontinent** called **Pangea**. Dinosaurs evolved and spread out across this supercontinent, during the **Triassic period**. That is why fossils of the same type of dinosaur can be found around the edges of the continents. Dinosaurs lived by the oceans, river banks, and in desert **oases** during Triassic times, and grazed on the branches of trees. In the **Jurassic period**, the **climate** got milder and moister, and more dinosaurs started to appear. These included bigger plant eaters—and the first giant meat eaters, the topic of this book.

Cretaceous Changes

Over time, Pangea began to split up and dinosaurs started to change.

Ceratosaurus ●
156-145 million
years ago

● Allosaurus
154-140 million
years ago

227 millions of years ago	205		180		159	
		Lower		Middle		Upper
TRIASSIC			JURASSIC			

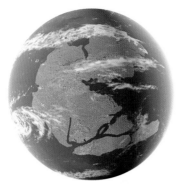

Triassic World Most of Earth's land is joined together in a single supercontinent.

Cretaceous World The supercontinent starts to split up.

By the end of the **Cretaceous period**, the dinosaurs that lived in North America looked very different from those in South America, and those in Europe, Asia, and Africa differed, too. **Vegetation** changed, too. Flowering plants had sprung up all over the world, and different types of dinosaurs adapted to eat them **evolved**.

Destruction!

Then, 65 million years ago, the dinosaurs were suddenly all wiped out.

Scientists think that this may have been caused by the impact of an enormous **meteor** that struck in Mexico. The only dinosaurs that survived were the bird-like dinosaurs, who were able to burrow, swim, or fly to escape the deadly effects of the meteor impact. After the dinosaurs came a new age—the age of the **mammals** (and that includes people).

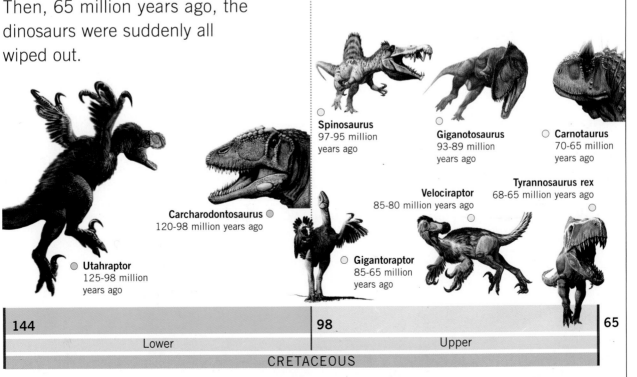

Spinosaurus
97-95 million
years ago

Giganotosaurus
93-89 million
years ago

Carnotaurus
70-65 million
years ago

Velociraptor
85-80 million years ago

Tyrannosaurus rex
68-65 million years ago

Carcharodontosaurus
120-98 million years ago

Utahraptor
125-98 million
years ago

Gigantoraptor
85-65 million
years ago

144		98		65
	Lower		Upper	
		CRETACEOUS		

Tyrannosaurus rex (ti-RAN-o-SAWR-us)

Tyrannosaurus rex (tyrant lizard king) was the king of the dinosaurs. As tall as a house, quick, and armed with a deadly bite, it was one of the scariest ever to walk the Earth.

🐾 LEGS

T-rex's legs were long and powerful. It was fast for such a big animal, but many smaller dinosaurs would have been quick enough to escape this monster.

🐾 FOOD

With its banana-sized teeth and bone-crushing bite, *T-rex* ate large **herbivores** such as this *Alamosaurus* (center). T-rex, a Cretaceous **carnivore,** also feasted on the remains of dead dinosaurs.

Dino-Data

Height	13 feet (4 m)
Length	41.9 feet (12.8 m)
Weight	1,764 lbs (6,800 kg)

Allosaurus (AL-o-SAWR-us)

Allosaurus (different lizard) was one of largest carnivores of the Jurassic period. It was lightly built, but very powerful. Its fossils have been found across the western United States, and also in Portugal.

🐾 CLAWS

Allosaurus had three fingers on each hand, each with huge claws. These 10 inch (25 cm) weapons were used to rip into the flesh of other dinosaurs.

Dino-Data

Height	13 feet (4 m)
Length	31.8 feet (9.7 m)
Weight	5,070 lbs (2,300 kg)

⏻ FOOD

As well as eating smaller animals, *Allosaurus* also hunted in packs to catch giant herbivores called **sauropods**.

⏻ TEETH

This carnivore had huge jaws with blade-like teeth to slice up meat. If a tooth broke off, another one grew back in its place.

Carcharodontosaurus
(kahr-KAR-o-DON-to-SAWR-us)

Carcharodontosaurus (shark-toothed lizard) was a gigantic carnivorous dinosaur that lived during the Cretaceous period. Fossils of this dinosaur have been found in North Africa. They show that its body was even longer than that of *Tyrannosaurus rex* (see pages 6–7).

🦴 SKULL

Carcharodontosaurus had long, sharp teeth and a huge skull. Despite this, though, it was not intelligent. It had a much smaller brain than *T-rex*.

Dino-Data

Height	23 feet (7 m)
Length	44 feet (13.5 m)
Weight	1,600 lbs (7,258 kg)

BALANCE

This North African dinosaur had a thick-set body, heavy bones, and a massive tail, which it used for balance. It could lumber after and catch big herbivores like this *Paralititan*.

Giganotosaurus (jig-a-NOT-o-SAWR-us)

Giganotosaurus (giant southern lizard) is the biggest meat eater ever discovered. It lived during the Cretaceous period. *Giganotosaurus* fossils were first found by a car mechanic in Argentina, whose hobby was looking for dinosaur bones!

☹ MOVEMENT

Giganotosaurus walked on two legs and could move at great speed. Its slim, pointed tail was used to provide balance and make quick turns while running.

☹ FOOD

Fossils of big plant eaters called Titanosaurs have been found near *Giganotosaurus* remains. This suggests this meat eater's **diet** included giant herbivores.

Dino-Data

Height	12.1 feet (3.7 m)
Length	43.3 feet (13.2 m)
Weight	17,636 lbs (8,000 kg)

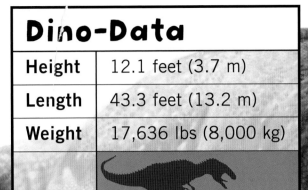

🌀 SENSE OF SMELL

The size of its **nostril cavity** suggests that *Giganotosaurus* had an extremely good sense of smell. It may have used this to sniff out dead animals many miles away.

Carnotaurus (KAHR-no-TAWR-us)

Carnotaurus (carnivorous bull) was a large meat-eating dinosaur that lived during the Cretaceous period. A single fossilized skeleton was found in Argentina in 1985.

Dino-Data

Height	13 feet (4 m)
Length	24.6 feet (7.5 m)
Weight	3,527 lbs (1,600 kg)

✔ HORNS

Carnotaurus had two thick horns above its eyes. It probably would have used these to fight with other males for the attention of a mate.

✔ SKIN

The *Carnotaurus* fossil shows that this dinosaur had skin lined with rows of bumps. It might have been able to change its appearance to blend in with the surroundings, like a chameleon.

Spinosaurus (SPINE-o-SAWR-us)

Spinosaurus (spine lizard) lived in North Africa during the Cretaceous period. The first remains found of this dinosaur were destroyed in World War II (1939–1945), but parts of its skull have been discovered in recent years.

✔ SAIL

Spinosaurus had a spiny sail that grew up to 6.5 feet (2 m) long. It was used to stop the dinosaur from getting too hot or too cold, to attract a mate, and to scare off other animals.

Dino-Data

Height	18.3 feet (5.6 m)
Length	45.9 feet (14 m)
Weight	17,637 lbs (8,000 kg)

✔ HEAD

The skull had a narrow snout filled with straight, smooth teeth. These were perfect for eating fish.

✔ CLAWS

Spinosaurus had a diet like that of a grizzly bear. It would have used its long, sharp claws to hook fish out of the water. It also feasted on smaller dinosaurs and the remains of dead animals.

Utahraptor (YOO-tah-RAP-tor)

Utahraptor (hunter of Utah) was a terrifying Cretaceous meat eater. Its fossils have been found in the United States. It was a lightly built, speedy, bird-like dinosaur.

LETHAL WEAPONS

Utahraptor had a huge curved claw on its second toe that could grow 9 inches (23 cm) long. It hunted by grasping its **prey** with its front legs while kicking at it with its back legs.

⚡ HUNTER

Utahraptor's long tail was used for balance and fast turning ability. Here it has hunted down a heavily armored plant eater called a *Gastonia*, ready for a fight to the death.

Dino-Data

Height	6.5 feet (2 m)
Length	23 feet (7 m)
Weight	1,543 lbs (700 kg)

Ceratosaurus (se-RAT-o-SAWR-us)

Ceratosaurus (horned lizard) was a large meat eater from the Late Jurassic period. Its fossils have been found in North America, Tanzania, and Portugal.

✔ FOOD

Ceratosaurus had a flexible body with a tail shaped like a crocodile's. This means it would have been a good swimmer and probably ate a fish-based diet.

Dino-Data

Height	8.2 feet (2.5 m)
Length	26 feet (8 m)
Weight	2,205 lbs (1,000 kg)

HEAD

Ceratosaurus had large jaws, dagger-like teeth and a blade-like horn on its snout. It had large eyes, which gave it good eyesight that allowed it to track prey from a distance.

Gigantoraptor (ji-GAN-to-RAP-tor)

Gigantoraptor (giant thief) was a huge, bird-like dinosaur that lived in Mongolia, near China, during the Cretaceous period. It looked similar to a turkey—but 35 times bigger! This monster was larger than the **tyrannosaur** *Alectrosaurus* (below), and would not have been easily frightened.

Dino-Data

Height	16.4 feet (5 m)
Length	26 feet (8 m)
Weight	3,086 lbs (1,400 kg)

☝ APPEARANCE

Gigantoraptor had a beak instead of toothed jaws. It probably had feathers, too. It hatched eggs in the same way that modern birds do.

☝ FOOD

Gigantoraptor had powerful back legs that allowed it to chase after its prey, and large, slashing claws that it could have used to rip into flesh.

Velociraptor (vee-LOHS-i-RAP-tor)

Velociraptor (swift hunter) was a ferocious, feathered meat eater. It lived during the Cretaceous period in Mongolia.

🦖 JAWS

Velociraptor had 28 teeth on each side. They were jagged at the back, making it easier to snatch and hold on to fast moving prey.

Dino-Data

Height	3.2 feet (1 m)
Length	6.5 feet (2 m)
Weight	33 lbs (15 kg)

✔ INTELLIGENCE

Velociraptor had one of the biggest brains relative to its size out of all the dinosaurs. This intelligent, cunning creature probably hunted in packs and may have killed very large dinosaurs.

✔ KILLING CLAWS

Velociraptor had a curved claw on each back foot. This 2.7 inch (7 cm) weapon was used to slash at other animals, while the claws on its hands gripped the prey.

QUIZ— Look back through the book to find the answers

TYRANNOSAURUS REX (ti-RAN-o-SAWR-us)

- How many fingers did *T-rex* have on each hand?
- Was *T-rex* the biggest meat-eating dinosaur?
- How long were *T-rex's* teeth?
- What does *Tyrannosaurus rex* mean?

ALLOSAURUS (AL-o-SAWR-us)

- What does the name *Allosaurus* mean?
- How long were its claws?
- What kind of food did it eat?
- When did *Allosaurus* live?

CARCHARODONTOSUARUS (kahr-KAR-o-DON-to-SAWR-us)

- What does the name *Carchardontosaurus* mean?
- Did it have a larger or smaller brain than *T-rex*?
- What kind of food did it eat?
- How big was this dinosaur's skull?

GIGANOTOSAURUS (jig-a-NOT-o-SAWR-us)

- What does the name *Giganotosaurus* mean?
- Was this dinosaur bigger or smaller than *T-rex*?
- What kind of food did it eat?
- Did *Giganotosaurus* have a good sense of smell?

CARNOTAURUS (KAHR-no-TAWR-us)

- What does the name *Carnotaurus* mean?
- Where have its fossils been found?
- What did *Carnotaurus's* skin look like?
- What period of time did this dinosaur live in?

SPINOSAURUS (SPINE-o-SAWR-us)

- What does the name *Spinosaurus* mean?
- What was the dinosaur's sail used for?
- What kind of diet did *Spinosaurus* have?
- What happened to the first fossils of *Spinosaurus*?

UTAHRAPTOR (YOO-tah-RAP-tor)

- What does the name *Utahraptor* mean?
- Where was *Utahraptor* discovered?
- How tall was *Utahraptor?*
- What other features did this dinosaur have?

CERATOSAURUS (se-RAT-o-SAWR-us)

- What does the name *Ceratosaurus* mean?
- Did *Ceratosaurus* have good eyesight?
- Where have its fossils been found?
- What other amazing features did this dinosaur have?

GIGANTORAPTOR (ji-GAN-to-RAP-tor)

- Where have fossils of *Gigantoraptor* been found?
- What kind of mouth did *Gigantoraptor* have?
- What does the name *Gigantoraptor* mean?
- Was *Gigantoraptor* a fast or slow dinosaur?

VELOCIRAPTOR (vee-LOHS-i-RAP-tor)

- What does the name *Velociraptor* mean?
- Did *Velociraptor* walk on two or four legs?
- *Velociraptor* had a special weapon on each foot. What was this weapon and what shape was it?
- What period of time did this dinosaur live in?

Glossary

Cambrian period: A period of time between 570–500 million years ago.

Carnivore: An animal that feeds on meat.

Climate: The temperature of a place.

Cretaceous period: A period of time between 144–65 million years ago.

Diet: The food an animal eats.

Dinosaur: An extinct reptile that lived during the Mesozoic era.

Era: A division of geological time.

Erosion: A gradual wearing away of rocks or soil.

Evolve: The developing of different kinds of lifeforms from earlier varieties.

Fossil: Remains or impressions of a prehistoric animal or plant embedded in rock.

Herbivore: An animal that only eats plants.

Jurassic period: A period of time between 180–144 million years ago.

Landmass: A continent or other large area of land.

Mammal: An animal that gives birth to live young.

Mesozoic era: A period of time between 230–65 million years ago.

Meteor: A rock from space.

Mineral: A naturally-formed substance. Minerals are the building blocks of rocks.

Nostril cavity: Area in the skull reponible for smell.

Oases: Small, green areas in a desert region, usually with water.

Pangea: The name given to the supercontinent that existed at the beginning of the age of the dinosaurs.

Prehistoric: Name given to the period of time before the arrival of humans.

Quarternary period: A period of time from 1.6 million years ago to the present day.

Reptile: A cold-blooded animal.

Rock: A naturally formed substance that makes up our Earth.

Sauropods: A group of large, four-legged, herbivorous dinosaurs. They had very long necks, small heads with blunt teeth, a small brain, and long tails that helped to balance their necks.

Supercontinent: The single landmass that existed at the time of the dinosaurs (see Pangea).

Titanosaur: A plant-eating dinosaur with a long, thin neck and a long, whiplike tail.

Triassic period : A period of time between 227–180 million years ago.

Tyrannosaur: A large, carnivorous dinosaur that lived in the Late Cretaceous period.

Vegetation: Plants that can be eaten.

Earth's Time Line

The history of the Earth dates back over 4.5 billion years. Scientists divide this time into periods. The earliest period of time is the **Cambrian period**. Dinosaurs appeared on Earth from the Triassic to the Cretaceous periods. Mammals, including humans, appeared in the **Quarternary period**.

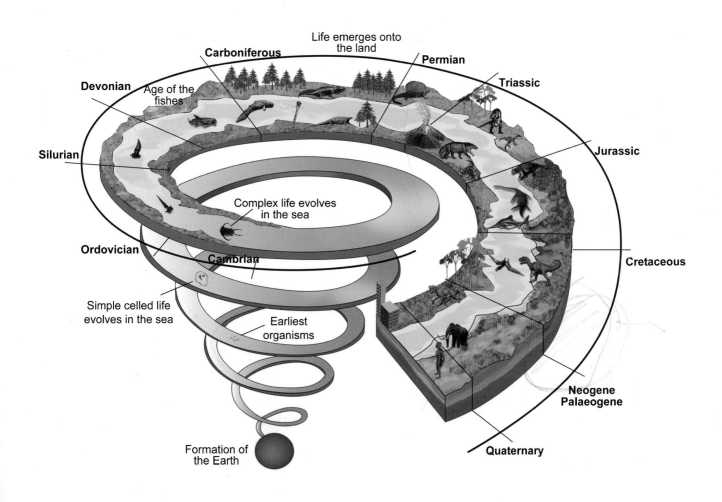

- Carboniferous
- Life emerges onto the land
- Permian
- Devonian
- Age of the fishes
- Triassic
- Silurian
- Jurassic
- Complex life evolves in the sea
- Ordovician
- Cambrian
- Cretaceous
- Simple celled life evolves in the sea
- Earliest organisms
- Neogene Palaeogene
- Formation of the Earth
- Quaternary

Index